TO

FROM

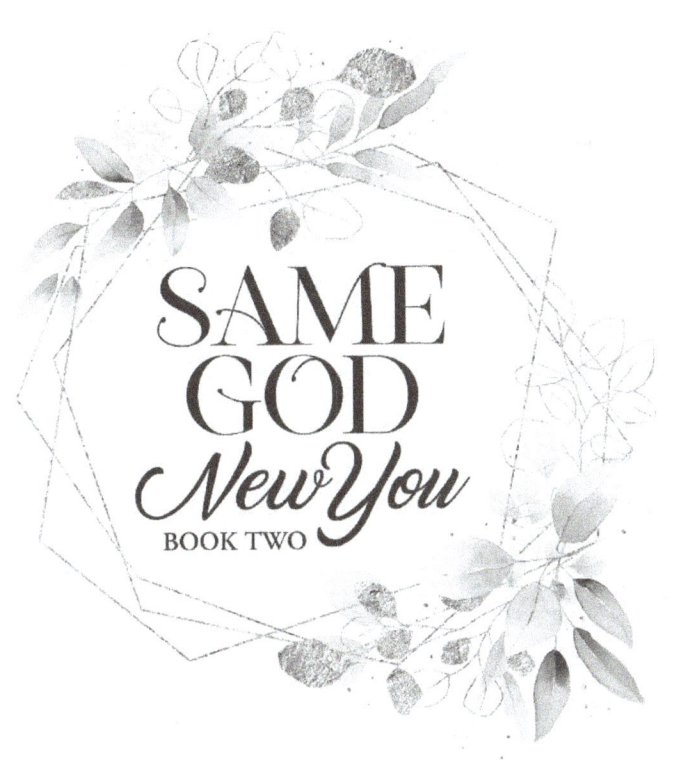

SAME GOD
New You
BOOK TWO

HOLLY JO FLORA

Same God, New You – Book Two

Copyright © 2025 by Holly Jo Flora

ISBN 979-8-9911567-3-8

Cover design: Julie May – Anything Creative
Interior design: Holly Jo Flora

10   9   8   7   6   5   4   3   2   1

TO ALEX

CONTENTS

Introduction

Welcome to *Same God, New You – Book Two*! If you've already read my first devotional, thank you for joining me again. The focus of this book is the same as book one: to help you grow in your faith and mature in your relationships.

I enjoy applicable teaching, real-life examples, and everyday situations. I'm a lover of practical application and down-to-earth thinking. I try to be kind and thoughtful with my words while also being straightforward and honest.

I'll share again what I wrote in my first devotional: You may not agree with everything I've written, and that's okay! God could be teaching you different lessons than He's teaching me. Your perspectives and experiences are different than mine, and I'll be the first to say that I absolutely do not know everything. But if what I share on these pages causes you to grow in any positive way, no matter how small, I'm delighted and honored that God used my words.

As you read *Same God, New You – Book Two*, please know I've been praying for you. I've asked God to use this book to bless and encourage you. I hope this devotional will help you grow in your relationship with Him and with others. Thank you for letting this book be a part of your journey.

ENJOYING EVERY AGE

This is the day that the LORD has made;
let us rejoice and be glad in it.

Psalm 118:24, ESV

Kayla is an amazing massage therapist and one of my dear friends. She owns a beautiful spa where I live. We usually chat for a bit before each of my appointments. During one of these catch-ups, we talked about how fast her kids and my kids were growing up. I remember saying to her, "But every age is so fun!"

A few minutes later during my massage, I kept hearing in my mind what I'd said to Kayla: *Every age is so fun.* What I meant, of course, was that every age my daughter and son had gone through had been so enjoyable. But I felt God ask me, "Are *you* enjoying every age?"

Was I enjoying *me* at every age? No. No, I was not. I was about to turn forty years old, and I felt disappointed in myself most of the time. I felt annoyed and embarrassed if my gray roots were showing. I was noticing more wrinkles on my forehead and a droopy spot on my left eyelid. My metabolism was slowing down, and I ate most meals with a side of guilt. I just felt like I was . . . failing at aging well . . . failing at aging gracefully. I was looking older.

I didn't want to feel like that any longer. Why was I upset with myself for getting older? I mean, I hadn't done anything wrong! Getting older isn't a bad thing, and it's also not something we can stop from happening.

I want to enjoy every age. I want my kids to see their mom enjoying herself at every age. So, I decided to make some changes in my life and see if that would help me feel better.

The first change I made was I stopped getting my hair colored. Now, please understand what I'm saying and what I'm *not* saying. I am not telling you to stop dyeing your hair. I went to the hair salon every five weeks for ten years so Mendy could color my grays away, and doing that made me happy. If coloring your hair makes you feel happy, go for it! But somewhere in my late thirties, dyeing my hair had started making me feel unhappy. I'd look in the mirror and see brown hair—similar to what I naturally had in my twenties—but then I'd look at my face under my brown hair, and my face did *not* look like it had in my twenties.

For me, I realized that I was chasing a look that was no longer "me." I decided to grow my gray-and-white hair out, and let me tell you, I have thoroughly enjoyed it! It has felt so freeing! This action helped me accept who I am, where I am, and what I look like at this age. Again, you and I are different people, and growing out your gray hair may not make you feel better. And that is completely fine.

The next thing I did was take all of the jeans and pants that no longer fit me out of my closet. I had almost twenty pairs of pants taking up valuable closet space—pants I hadn't worn in years but, for some reason, had held on to. Every time I walked into my closet and saw those pants, I felt guilty because they no longer fit. I felt like me changing was me failing. The day I decided to stop coloring my hair, I went into my closet, grabbed all those pants, put them into bags, and donated them. I felt so much better!

I didn't "give up on myself" by doing those things. No, I just stopped chasing what I used to be, because I want to enjoy who and how I am right now. I want to be healthy, of course. I still exercise, try to make healthy food choices, take vitamins, drink water, get facials, and use my face serums. But I also want to enjoy myself at every age, just like I enjoy my kids, and I want them to see me enjoying every age. I think that is truly what "aging gracefully" means.

Now, at almost forty-two, I am looking at myself with much kinder eyes than I did when I was thirty-nine. I'm enjoying myself more. I hope you are enjoying yourself at every age too. Never forget: You are fearfully and wonderfully made . . . at every age.

I praise you because I am fearfully and wonderfully made; your works are wonderful, I know that full well.

Psalm 139:14, NIV

PRAYER PROMPTS FOR TODAY

~ Are you struggling with aging or changing? If you are, pray for God to help you find joy where you are right now.

~ Do you have loved ones who are unhappy with themselves? Pray for them. Ask God to show you how you can encourage them.

I, Not We

I can do all things through
Christ who strengthens me.

Philippians 4:13, NKJV

A friend of ours passed away less than two weeks before Christmas. The day after his funeral, I was addressing our Christmas cards. I came to his and his wife's address on my list. It felt so weird and sad to put only her name on the card. It struck me right then how difficult it would be for her every time she reached into her mailbox that December and pulled out cards addressed to only her, each one a reminder that her loving husband was no longer physically with her.

Death changes everything about your life, including how you talk. You no longer say "we" and "us." It's now "I" and "me."

One of the most encouraging verses in the Bible for anyone who's experienced the death of a spouse is Philippians 4:13: "I can do all things through Christ who strengthens me." Notice the first and last words of that verse: *I* and *me*. It doesn't say *we* and *us*. This verse speaks to each of us individually. This verse is for you.

Let's look at each part of Philippians 4:13. We've already acknowledged the first word, *I*, so let's move on to the next part, *can*. Notice the word is *can* and not *will*. *Can* is not a guarantee, because we see people every day who *can* but don't. *Can* tells us that we have a part to play in the outcome. *Can* means you have a choice.

Now, let's look at the word *do*. *Do* is an action verb. *Do* tells us that in order to claim this verse as our own, we must choose to take action, choose to *do* what pleases God.

The next words are *all things*. These words tell us that we can accomplish small things, big things, and everything in between. Doing *all things* can feel overwhelming or even scary when you're alone, but the last part of the verse explains how you'll be able to do it: "through Christ who strengthens me."

You may feel a bit powerless alone, but you're not. God is always with you, and He will empower you for everything He's called you to do. God will supply your needs, and He will direct you. My pastor, Roger Graham, says, "Where He guides, He will provide!"

And my God will meet all your needs according to the riches of his glory in Christ Jesus.

Philippians 4:19, NIV

Notice that in Philippians 4:19, we have the word *will*—not *can*, not *may*. *Will* is a guarantee. God *will* meet your needs according to His riches, and His riches are endless!

Trust God and obey Him. When you do that, He will pour His riches—strength, comfort, wisdom, power, love, peace, guidance, and blessings—into you until you are overflowing.

PRAYER PROMPTS FOR TODAY

~ Pray for people who've experienced the death of a spouse.

~ Ask God to show you ways to encourage and support your loved ones who are feeling alone. Be sure to take action with any ideas He gives you.

~ If you have experienced the death of a spouse, apply Philippians 4:13 to the situations you face. Make the verse personal to you. You may want to replace "all things" with a specific circumstance you're struggling with. Here are a few examples:

"I can go out to eat by myself through Christ who strengthens me."

"I can sign only my name on cards through Christ who strengthens me."

"I can go back to my Sunday school class without my spouse through Christ who strengthens me."

"I can have a bright, beautiful future through Christ who strengthens me."

* My pastor, Roger Graham, preached a sermon in 2023 that inspired this devotion. Thank you, Brother Roger, for teaching us the Word.

3

WE'RE TOUGH!

*Now what I am commanding you today is not
too difficult for you or beyond your reach.*

Deuteronomy 30:11, NIV

Madelyn, Derek, and I were driving to church—
Alex was already there for band practice. We
passed a tree where half of the tree had broken off
and was lying on the ground.

Derek said, "Oh, Mom! Look! What happened

to that tree?"

"I'm not sure. Lots of things could have done that. Maybe the tree had a disease," I answered.

Derek then asked what a disease was. Before I could answer him, Madelyn said, "Derek, *we* have a disease. Cystic fibrosis is a disease."

"It is?" Derek asked.

"Yeah, and you can die from CF," said Madelyn.

I caught my breath. See, Alex and I had never told Madelyn or Derek that CF is a terminal disease. We didn't want to scare them. We always knew that we'd need to have those talks with them at some point. We'd just been answering their questions as they asked them, and so far, they'd never asked us if cystic fibrosis could kill them.

Then Madelyn said this, and y'all . . . I just can't even. She said, "But you and I are *not* going to die from it. CF isn't tough for us. *We're* tough for CF."

And as I drove, I fist-bumped the air!

I am a firm believer that our attitude affects not only our day but our health as well. We all face situations that are uncomfortable, draining, and even scary at times, but let us never forget to tap into the strength offered to us from the Lord.

You may be feeling weak today. You might be running on empty. You could be exhausted from what you're facing. You may feel defeated. Maybe you're scared. Please know that through Christ, you are strong! You are brave! My friend, you are tough!

Yet in all these things we are more than conquerors through Him who loved us.

Romans 8:37, NKJV

Prayer Prompts for Today

~ Have you been feeling weak and defeated? Ask God to give you His strength, fill you with positive energy, clothe you in His armor, and give you an attitude of boldness.

IT'S NOT TOO LATE

Every time I think of you, I give thanks to my God. Whenever I pray, I make my requests for all of you with joy . . .

Philippians 1:3-4, NLT

We have dear friends who have a pool. Every summer, they bless our family by letting us come and swim any time we like. But their gift goes further than just that. Pools can grow *Pseudomonas aeruginosa*, a bacteria that is dangerous to our children's health. On the days that our family plans to swim, our friends have their pool water tested for pseudomonas, and those tests are expensive. On our pool day mornings, I always get the text "Pool water is safe" with a picture of a pseudomonas test strip—every single time.

We never asked them to do this. They do it because they're incredibly caring people who love us. They researched cystic fibrosis issues with pools all on their own. They chose to not only give us the gift of "pool days" but to also give us the gift of less worry. We are so blessed to have them in our lives.

One day, Alex, the kids, and I were sitting by our friends' pool. We were eating oranges during our snack break. Derek asked me if I got to swim a lot when I was a kid. I told him that when I was little, there was a lady who went to church with my grandma. Her name was Mrs. Sarah. She lived less than a mile from my house. Mrs. Sarah told my parents that my sister and I were welcome to come swim at her house anytime we'd like. As a child, I had so much fun swimming in Mrs. Sarah's pool. I have lots of great memories.

When we finished eating our oranges, Alex, Madelyn, and Derek jumped back into the pool. I stayed on the lounge chair to read a book, but I wasn't able to read much. My mind stayed on Mrs. Sarah.

I sat beside the pool and thought about how

kind that was of her. For years, that sweet lady let my family use her pool, and I couldn't remember us ever doing anything nice for her as a thank-you. We never mowed her yard, baked her a cake, mailed her a thank-you card, or sent her flowers. That realization bothered me.

Thankfully, it wasn't too late. The next day, I found Mrs. Sarah on Facebook. I sent her this message:

> Mrs. Sarah, some of our friends let us swim in their pool every summer. Yesterday, we were at their pool, and I was telling my kids about fun memories I have of swimming in your pool when I was little. Thank you so much for letting Manda and me come over to swim when we were kids! We truly had the best time!

It is never too late to say "Thank you."

PRAYER PROMPTS FOR TODAY

~ Think of people in your life now who go out of their way to show you kindness. Thank God for them, and ask Him to bless them and their families.

~ Think of people who were kind to you when you were a kid. Ask God to bless them. Ask Him how you can show your appreciation. He may direct you to send a message, make a call, or mail a card. Please be obedient.

~ If the person you want to thank has passed away, pray about reaching out to their family. Sharing good memories and a grateful heart with the person's loved ones is a wonderful way of showing your appreciation!

~ Pray for God to show you how you can be kind to the people in your life. Your kindness could create memories for them that last their lifetime!

Real Is Not Controversial

*Therefore each of you must put off falsehood
and speak truthfully to your neighbor, for
we are all members of one body.*

Ephesians 4:25, NIV

When I published *Same God, New You* in May of
2023, I knew God had plans for the devotional, but
I had no idea what those plans were. I bathed that
book release day in prayer, hoping the words God

had given me would be a blessing to readers and spread all over the world! I pray for big things.

I wanted to do my part in marketing the book and getting the message out there. One of the ideas I had was to contact Christian book publishers and Christian influencers. I mailed them more copies of *Same God, New You* than I can count. I would either get no reply back or, when I did, I'd receive practically the same message. I'll put their feedback in a nutshell: My book contained many controversial topics—like divorce, terminal disease, and autism—and they did not think their readers/followers/viewers would be interested or approve.

Before I continue, let me just say that I do *not* think my devotional topics are controversial. I believe they are just *life* topics that all people have to deal with. Christians are people. We are not immune to these subjects. We should not feel uncomfortable or unallowed to discuss them.

Their responses were, of course, discouraging but also confusing, because at the same time I was getting their feedback, I was also receiving the sweetest messages from you wonderful readers—messages like "I relate to every devotion!" and "I read the whole book in one day because I couldn't put it down!" I was also checking the book sales every day and seeing copy after copy sell.

I don't think some Christian influencers and publishers know us all as well as they think they do. I also think they are doing the Christian community a disservice and, most importantly, displeasing God if they're promoting an idea that certain topics and conversations are off-limits for Christians. These subjects and discussions are found all throughout Scripture. Jesus didn't shy away from conversations with real people. Ladies, that's what we all are, believers or not: We are all just real people who go through real life, difficult situations.

Please take these words to heart. If you've had an affair, battled addiction, questioned your faith, been an atheist, or made choices you regret, we *want* to hear your redemption story. God can use your past, present, and future for His glory. Please do not ever feel that you should keep quiet about your "controversial" life because it is *not* controversial. Your life is a *real* life because you are a *real* person—a woman whom God loves.

Prayer Prompts for Today

~ Thank God for bringing you through the difficult situations you've faced.

~ If you are still "in the thick of it," ask God to help you. Pray for His strength, guidance, wisdom, and peace.

~ Pray that God will help you be a person others feel comfortable sharing their past with.

A Rock in the Drawer

Continue earnestly in prayer, being
vigilant in it with thanksgiving . . .

Colossians 4:2, NKJV

My sister-in-law keeps a rock in one of her bathroom drawers. Why? So that every time she sees the rock, she's reminded to pray over a stressful situation.

I love the purposefulness of her action. She

wants peace so much over this situation that she refuses to let herself forget to pray over it. She will not allow herself to slack on taking the need to God. I also love that she placed this rock where most likely no one else will ever see it. She didn't put the rock there "for show." No, this is just her personal reminder to pray daily over the situation.

Are you struggling with circumstances that you desperately wish would change? Are you seeking reconciliation in a strained relationship? Are you dealing with consequences from a choice you regret? You, too, may want to go outside, pick up a rock, and place it in a drawer. Choose a drawer you open daily, and every time you see that rock, pray over your situation. Some days, you may say a long prayer, while other days, you may only have time to breathe a few quick words, and that's absolutely fine. Pray and watch God do what only He can do.

PRAYER PROMPTS FOR TODAY

~ Oftentimes, when praying for God to change a situation in our lives, we tell God what we want Him to do. If you've prayed this way in the past, you may want to change your approach. Ask God to handle your situation however He sees fit and make the desires of your heart match His will.

SILENT

*Every day I call to you, my God, but you
do not answer. Every night I lift my
voice, but I find no relief.*

Psalm 22:2, NLT

When I was in school, I took lots of tests. For the
larger, more important exams, I remember my
teachers were silent. They stayed in the room with
us during the tests, but they wouldn't answer any

of our questions.

Have you ever gone through a difficult test in life and felt that God was remaining silent during it? You pray and beg God for help, but you feel your cries are met with silence? Please remember: The Teacher stays silent during important tests. But just because He's silent, that does not mean He is absent. No, He is right there with you, cheering you on and hoping you'll remember all He's taught you.

"God has not been trying an experiment on my faith or love in order to find out their quality. He knew it already. It was I who didn't." - C.S. Lewis[1]

PRAYER PROMPTS FOR TODAY

~ If you feel that God is staying silent, please know there is a reason. In His wisdom, God knows exactly what He is doing and why. Trust Him. Don't stop praying. Keep reading your Bible. Listen to Christian music. Remember: His silence does not mean He isn't with you. He is, and He loves you.

8

DISTRACTED

A new command I give you: Love one another.
As I have loved you, so you must love one
another. By this everyone will know that you
are my disciples, if you love one another.

John 13:34-35, NIV

I used to be a Facebook fighting warrior. When I saw a post I disagreed with, I'd roll my sleeves up and forcefully start typing out a lecture—I mean, a comment. Unfortunately, in trying to prove my point, the only point I frequently proved was that I could be rude. Did I really think my harsh comments would change anyone's opinions?

One morning while driving to work, I heard a radio commentor share about this very topic. He said that as Christians, we've become distracted in our mission. He pointed out that so many times, we think it's *our* responsibility to change people's minds, but it's not. God has called us to lovingly share the Gospel. Once a person accepts Christ and becomes a Christian, God changes their heart, and then, as a result, their thinking eventually changes too.

Nonbelievers should not be expected to think or make decisions like believers do. People who do not know the Lord have a different moral compass and foundation than Christians. Nonbelievers are more apt to make decisions and form beliefs based on personal logic and what's socially acceptable, as we're all tempted to do. But Christians are called to make decisions based on God's teachings.

A Christian's main goal is to spread the Gospel, but we are so easily distracted. You know who loves that? Satan. Satan loves when we argue about politics. He's thrilled when we lecture on morality. He's giddy when we give unsolicited advice.

Why does Satan love when we do that? Because we often get so worked up and judgmental that we forget to tell others about what Jesus did for them and His love for them—we forget to actually witness! And if we *do* remember to share the Gospel, nonbelievers typically don't listen to or believe us—understandably so, since they've mainly felt hostility from Christians. They have felt insulted and condemned by believers. What they have *not* felt from us is love. The Bible tells us that others will know we are God's disciples by our *love*.

We can't change people's minds—only God can do that. We are simply commanded to love and tell others about Jesus. When nonbelievers truly meet our Savior, He—and only He—can change their hearts and minds.

Prayer Prompts for Today

~ Do you frequently find yourself arguing with and lecturing people? If so, ask God to help you focus instead on loving others.

~ Pray for God to give you opportunities to share His love—to share the Gospel. Be prepared. Satan will try to distract you. Stay focused and remember that only God can change a person's heart and mind.

WHEN IT DOESN'T MAKE SENSE

When I am afraid, I put my trust in you.
In God, whose word I praise—in God
I trust and am not afraid.

Psalm 56:3-4a, NIV

I was listening to *The Message* in my car this morning, and the host made the most amazing statement. She said, "When it doesn't make sense, let it make faith." That. Is. Incredible.

I can be a Chatty Cathy. I can easily make a word salad. I'm in awe of people who can take a powerful lesson and present it to us in such a concise, well-thought-out sentence. *When it doesn't make sense, let it make faith.* Even as I type that statement, I want to yell, "Wooo!" and fist-bump the air!

We all go through situations where we cannot make sense of why God allowed what happened to happen. We just can't understand. The pain, fear, and turmoil we're experiencing feel overwhelming. Thoughts of *It didn't have to be this way!* or *Why did He allow this to happen?* can consume our minds.

In those moments, when we truly do not understand, we can *choose* to trust God—to trust that He knows best, has a plan, is in control, and will make all things work together for good. Choosing to trust God may not always be an easy choice. It's a decision that has to be made consciously over and over, but every time we choose to trust Him, our faith grows. As it grows, the choice to trust God can become a beautiful, comforting habit that we can lean into.

When we choose to trust God when things don't make sense, He pours His peace upon us—a peace that passes all understanding. The world around us can be absolutely falling apart, but we feel safe and secure in the loving arms of our Savior because we trust Him.

When it doesn't make sense,
let it make faith.

Prayer Prompts for Today

~ Are you experiencing a situation that doesn't make sense? Ask God to help you trust Him. Pray that through your circumstances, your faith will grow.

10

Mrs. Faye

And let us consider how to stir up one another to love and good works, not neglecting to meet together, as is the habit of some, but encouraging one another, and all the more as you see the Day drawing near.

Hebrews 10:24-25, ESV

When I was a teenager, a few of my friends and I prepared two songs to share at one of our church's Sunday evening services. Both of the songs were current (for the late nineties) worship songs. Our church typically only sang hymns. Other than choir soundtracks or special music where the singer played guitar, only piano and organ were used to accompany singing. My friends and I were a little anxious about sharing the music we loved with our church because we were playing drums, bass, piano, and guitar with our not-from-the-hymnbook songs.

The Sunday evening service came, and we nervously sang and played our two songs. We sounded . . . rough. Our nerves took over our voices and hands. There were many mistakes, but we did our best. Some of the facial expressions of people in the congregation let us know that not everyone was fond of our music, and let me tell you, it is hard to fully commit and try to minister when you're met with disapproving expressions.

After the service, many youth and young adults said kind words to us. I don't remember any older adults speaking to me except for one: Mrs. Faye Moon.

Mrs. Faye was an elderly woman in our church. She was petite and soft-spoken and had snow-white hair. She always had on a beautiful dress.

Mrs. Faye walked over to me and with the sweetest smile said, "Holly Jo, I so enjoyed the music tonight! I've never heard those songs before, but the lyrics were so true."

I hugged and thanked her. Mrs. Faye then went

to each of my friends and said kind words to them as well. My friends and I sang many more times at our church, and after each service, Mrs. Faye always came over and encouraged us.

Mrs. Faye was truly one of the sweetest, most loving women. She is the only person I've met so far that I can make this statement about: In all the years I knew her, I never heard her say one negative thing about anyone or anything.

Mrs. Faye always seemed to have her focus on the right place. It would have been so easy for her to focus on our bad notes, loud drums, and unfamiliar songs, but she always chose to focus on loving us—on encouraging us.

I hope every church has at least one Mrs. Faye. I hope you, dear reader, have a Mrs. Faye in your life, someone who leaves your cup full. I also hope you will *be* a Mrs. Faye to those around you. When we find ourselves in situations that aren't our cup of tea—moments that don't fit in with our tastes—I pray we'll all remember Mrs. Faye and how she always chose to point out the good.

Prayer Prompts for Today

~ Do you have a Mrs. Faye in your life? Take some time to pray for that person. You may want to write a card or send a message thanking them for how they encourage you.

~ Are you a Mrs. Faye to others? If not, ask God to help you see and praise the good in people.

HE WAITED TO EAT
HIS WAFFLES

Show hospitality to one another without grumbling.

1 Peter 4:9, ESV

A friend of mine once asked me, "When did you know that Alex was the one for you?"

I answered, "When he waited to eat his waffles."

One night after church, I went out to eat with a

large group of my friends. I was twenty-two years old and had a huge crush on Alex. To my delight, we sat next to each other at the Huddle House that night. I wasn't feeling very hungry, so I only ordered french fries. Alex ordered waffles.

When the waitress brought the food to our table, my french fries weren't there. She apologized and told me that she'd let the cook know. One of our friends prayed over the food, and everyone started eating . . . everyone except Alex.

He just kept talking and laughing with me and others at the table. But he never took a bite of his waffles. For some reason, my fries took about fifteen minutes to get to the table. I put ketchup on my plate, and as I lifted my first fry to my mouth, I saw out of the corner of my eye Alex take his first bite of his (had to be cold) waffles.

He never said anything about waiting to eat that night, but I saw it. I noticed, and I felt special. Soon after that meal at Huddle House, we started dating. The next year, we were engaged, and the year after that, we got married.

Alex still makes sacrifices, both small and large, for me. He also still doesn't complain or make a big show about doing them. He never brings them up. But I see them. I notice, and I still feel special.

I see God in my husband. I'm so thankful that my relationship with Alex has encouraged me to try to notice kindnesses, no matter how small. This has helped me see the love God displays for me every day and the love that others give.

Do you notice small acts of kindness? We all get busy and can sometimes miss things, but on a typical day, do you notice? The man who holds the door open for you, the woman at the drive-through who says, "Have a nice day," the child who smiles from ear to ear when they see you . . . Do you notice? Do you thank them? Do you thank God *for* them?

Let's thank God for the people in our lives who wait to eat their waffles. Let's also be people who let our waffles get cold without complaint.

Prayer Prompts for Today

~ Thank God for the people who showed you kindness this week.

~ Ask Him to help you look for opportunities and ways that you can show love to others.

ALL TALK

All hard work brings a profit,
but mere talk leads only to poverty.

Proverbs 14:23, NIV

When I became a mom, I made a decision that I never want my children to ever think I'm "all talk." I wanted them to know that if I said I was going to do something, I was going to do it! And I try to live that out from my huge announcements all the way down to my small statements, like "I'm not going to eat another cookie."

This truly is a strong conviction of mine because kids are watching. They hear what we say and then watch us to see if we really meant what we said. If they see us repeatedly saying things and then not following through, they may absorb the bad habit and grow up to be "all talk" too.

If you've had a person in your life who constantly said things they never followed through on, you know firsthand how people being "all talk" can cause you to lose respect for them. Also, listening to the same statements over and over when nothing ever changes can be exhausting and aggravating.

We can have the best of intentions and the most wonderful plans, but intentions and plans don't get things done. While well-thought-out preparation is very helpful and wise, at some point, we must leave the planning stage and get to the doing stage. We must take action. We must put feet to our words. The doing stage may involve a lot of hard work, but if God has called you to do it, you *can* do it! Try your hardest. Do your best. Your diligent work will not only lead to blessings but will also show others that you are not "all talk."

*But be doers of the word, and not
hearers only, deceiving yourselves.
James 1:22, NKJV*

*Whatever you do, work at it with all
your heart, as working for the LORD,
not for human masters . . .*

Colossians 3:23, NIV

I'll leave you with the wisdom I found inside the wrapper of my delicious Dove chocolate: "Don't just talk about it, be about it."

PRAYER PROMPTS FOR TODAY

~ Do you have statements you've repeated over and over that you've never followed through on? If God has called you to make those plans, then get started! Today is the day!

~ If you're unsure of why you've not been able to put feet to words before, ask God to reveal to you what's held you back in the past. Ask Him to help you take action.

WELCOME

*And whoever welcomes one such child
in my name welcomes me.*

Matthew 18:5, NIV

I had the most amazing youth pastor when I was a teenager. John and his wife, Debbie, were such loving leaders. They focused on making our youth group a welcoming environment. Not only did they display that welcoming spirit to every young person, but they also took the time to teach us about including others.

I remember during my last year of high school, John gathered all of the seniors together and told us that as the leaders of our youth group, he expected us to look for new young people in our church every Wednesday and Sunday. He encouraged us to go to visitors, introduce ourselves, and invite them to sit with us. He taught us lessons on how to speak to and include others. Because of John and Debbie, we had the most loving, welcoming youth group. I wish all teens could experience that kind of environment.

Occasionally, welcoming environments do "just happen." But most of the time, welcoming environments are created by loving individuals who truly *see* other people. Seeing others comes naturally to some people, but for those who aren't instinctively aware of others' emotions, it must be taught. John and Debbie taught us to focus on others.

Are we teaching our children and teens to actively include others? Do we tell our children that we expect them to welcome others into their group? Do we ask them if they sat by or spoke to someone new in their youth group? Also, are *we* showing younger generations this behavior by including others ourselves?

Christians should be the most welcoming people, and churches should be the most welcoming environments in the world. Please bring the wel-coming love of God with you everywhere you go. Like John and Debbie, your love and care for others can spread and help create an environ-ment where others feel welcome.

PRAYER PROMPTS FOR TODAY

~ Ask God to help you focus more on others. Pray that He will give you opportunities to make people feel seen and welcome.

THE WIDOW'S LESSONS
PART 1

The wife of a man from the company of the prophets cried out to Elisha, "Your servant my husband is dead, and you know that he revered the Lord. But now his creditor is coming to take my two boys as his slaves."

Elisha replied to her, "How can I help you? Tell me, what do you have in your house?"

"Your servant has nothing there at all,"
she said, "except a small jar of olive oil."

Elisha said, "Go around and ask all your
neighbors for empty jars. Don't ask for just a
few. Then go inside and shut the door behind
you and your sons. Pour oil into all the jars,
and as each is filled, put it to one side."

She left him and shut the door behind her and
her sons. They brought the jars to her and
she kept pouring. When all the jars were full,
she said to her son, "Bring me another one."

But he replied, "There is not a jar left."
Then the oil stopped flowing.

She went and told the man of God, and he
said, "Go, sell the oil and pay your debts.
You and your sons can live on what is left."

2 Kings 4:1-7, NIV

This story of the widow and the jars is one of my favorites in the Bible. The lessons we can learn from this passage are numerous—so numerous that I've broken this devotion into several parts. Let's jump into part 1.

The first lesson we can learn is where to go when we need guidance. When the woman found herself in a scary situation where she had no idea of what to do next, she went to a man of God. She did not jump on social media and ask advice. She didn't go to a gossip circle and ask opinions. No, she went to Elisha.

Where should you go when you need advice? First, pray and read your Bible. James 1:5 tells us to ask God for wisdom and that He will give it to us generously. That wisdom may lead you to talk to your pastor, your Sunday school teacher, or a friend who you know has wise counsel and follows God.

The second lesson we can learn is to start with what we have. After the widow presented her problem to Elisha, he asked her, "What do you have in your house?"

When tackling a problem, you may feel like what you have isn't enough. You may think: *I'm not smart enough to figure this out. I'm not talented enough for this to work. I don't have enough resources to make this happen.* And you know what? You may be right. On your own, you might not have enough, but God loves to take what we have and make it be enough. With God, all things are possible. When we give the little amount we have to God, He multiplies it. He turns not enough into overflowing!

The third lesson we can learn is that *we* have to do the work. I like how Elisha had the widow do the work. He didn't show up at her house with a bunch of empty jars that he'd gathered for her. No, she had to go and gather the jars herself.

Honestly, we live in a pretty lazy world, don't we? We'd all love to just wake up one morning to a living room filled with jars. God performed a miracle and put all these empty jars into our house for us to use—who wouldn't love that? And sometimes, He may do something like that, but most of the time, God wants us to go out and collect the jars.

Gathering the jars was tough work. The widow didn't have an air-conditioned car. She had to walk from house to house asking for jars. Then she had to carry those jars all the way back to her home. She had to do this again and again until she'd collected all the jars she could find. Elisha told her, "Don't ask for just a few." It was hard work. The tasks God gives you may also require hard work. If you're like me, I often pray for God to please bless the work I'm doing. We must remember that we can't ask Him to bless our work if we're not willing to actually *do* the work.

PRAYER PROMPTS FOR TODAY

~ Are you facing a situation that you have no idea how to handle? Pray. Ask God for wisdom. Read your Bible. God may lead you to speak to an Elisha.

~ Do you have a task that you must complete,

but you don't feel like you're enough? Pray for God to turn your "not enough" into overflowing!

~ Ask God to help you be a hard worker and to bless your efforts.

15

THE WIDOW'S LESSONS
PART 2

The fourth lesson we can learn is to gather as many jars as we can, even when there is no extra oil yet to be seen. When I first felt God calling me to write a book, I prayed every night, "Please, God, give me the opportunity, and I'll write the book." I was completely willing to write, but I was scared and felt lost because I didn't know what to do with a manuscript once I had it written. I wanted to first have a publishing plan or offer before I wrote my first devotional.

I prayed that prayer, "God, please give me the opportunity, and I'll write the book," for over a year. Then one night, I felt God say, "Holly Jo, write the book, and then I'll give you the opportunity." And so, I started writing, and God was true to His word.

God is pleased when we step out in faith to do what He's called us to do, especially when we have no visible guarantee for us to lean on. When all we have is God's promise and His leading—that nudge we feel in our spirit that lets us know what God wants us to do—and we're obedient, God's blessings overflow!

This widow wasn't sent a delivery email telling her that fifty gallons of oil would be delivered to her house tomorrow morning. No, all she had was the word of God through Elisha that if she gathered the jars, God would then send her the oil she so desperately needed. This shows us her faith. She didn't just gather two jars so that she could test it out—you know, pour from her tiny jar and see if it really would fill those two, and then if it did, she'd run out and grab some more. If she'd done that, she would have ended up with only two jars of oil because the Bible tells us that when there were no jars left in her house, the oil stopped. How much oil God pours out onto us is up to Him, but I for one don't want to miss out on His blessings because I didn't bring enough jars to hold them.

The fifth lesson we can learn is that we need to include younger generations. Many of us don't tell children enough about what God has done for us. Sometimes we don't even involve them in the work of God. What this creates is a generation who may believe that the God of the Bible could do miracles—but only back in Bible times, not now. Then they see Bible stories as outdated fairy tales.

Elisha told the widow to include her sons in the miracle. This woman's sons never forgot the day when they kept bringing empty jars to their mom and she kept pouring oil into them from a tiny jar. Her boys never forgot how God performed a miracle that allowed them to not be slaves. Her boys were there, handing their mom jars, watching the miracle happen right before their eyes.

The last lesson we can learn is that God can change everything. The Bible tells us in verse 7 that from selling the oil, she had not only enough money to pay off the debt and keep her boys, but she and her sons had enough to live on what was left. Only God could do that. This should give all of us hope.

I don't know what your life looks like today, but think about this woman. We don't know what day of the week the events in this passage occurred on, but let's pretend that on a Monday, the woman found out the creditor was going to take her sons to be his slaves to repay her husband's debt. Can you imagine how overcome with despair she must have been? How distraught she had to feel? She was already grieving the loss of her husband, and now this—she's going to lose both of her boys! They're going to be slaves, and she can't do anything in her own power to stop it from happening.

But let's say on Tuesday morning, she went to talk to Elisha. He tells her to collect the jars, fill them with oil, and sell them. Then on Tuesday night, this woman finds herself not only able to keep her sons, but she realizes that she'll never have to work another day of her life. She's financially set. From the despair the widow felt on Monday to the overflowing joy she felt on Tuesday—only God could do that!

Satan loves to get ahold of your thinking on the Monday night. When there seems to be no solution and you're sick with worry, Satan loves to whisper to you that things will never get any better, life will always be this hard. He tells you that you've messed up so much and it can never be fixed. Do not believe him. Give the situation you're in to God. Obey what He tells you to do, and watch your Monday turn into Tuesday!

Prayer Prompts for Today

~ Has God called you to do something but you've not started the project yet? If God is leading you to do this work, trust Him, and get started! Pray and ask God to guide your steps and bless your efforts.

~ Do you share what God has done or is doing in your life with your children, nieces, nephews, grandchildren, or the youth in your church? If not, ask God to give you opportunities to share your testimony with younger generations.

~ Are you facing a "Monday night"? Pray. Give the situation to God. Ask Him to turn your despair into joy!

16

SHUT THE DOOR

Elisha said, "Go around and ask all your neighbors for empty jars. Don't ask for just a few. Then go inside and shut the door behind you and your sons. Pour oil into all the jars, and as each is filled, put it to one side." She left him and shut the door behind her and her sons. They brought the jars to her and she kept pouring.

2 Kings 4:3-5, NIV

Let's look once more at 2 Kings chapter 4. In the story of the widow's olive oil, Elisha tells the woman to gather empty jars from her neighbors. He then gives her very specific directions. She is to take the jars into her house with her sons and shut the door. Why did Elisha tell her to shut the door? I believe it was for two reasons: to shut out the naysayers and to eliminate distractions.

When I wrote my first devotional, I "shut the door." I spent about five years writing the devotions in *Same God, New You*. The day I published the devotional was the same day that people found out I'd been writing a book. This goes completely against what we're told to do when marketing a new book. I built no hype for the book. I did no campaigns. There was no countdown to release day. But still, God blessed.

I knew I needed to write that first book without the pressures of others knowing what I was doing. I didn't want people asking me about my writing or giving me advice or criticism. I knew God had called me to write that devotional, and I was afraid that other people's thoughts, views, and questions might distract or discourage me.

This woman didn't need the distraction of people looking in her door and asking her what she was doing with all those jars. Then after she explained to them what Elisha had told her to do, she didn't need to hear, "That'll never work! You're crazy! You can't fill all those jars with that tiny amount of oil!"

When we don't "shut the door," we sometimes listen more to other people than we do to God.

I find it interesting that the author of 2 Kings chapter 4 wrote the phrase "shut the door" not once but twice. In verse 4, we're told that Elisha instructs the woman to "shut the door," and then the very next verse tells us the woman left Elisha and "shut the door" behind her and her sons. Why is the phrase "shut the door" used twice in this short passage? When details are repeated in scripture, it typically means that the message is important and needs to be emphasized. So, why is shutting the door significant? By shutting the door, this woman was able to stay focused on her motives and goal. She wasn't seeking attention or fame. She simply wanted to keep her boys.

Shutting the door is the opposite of what our culture encourages us to do. If this widow had lived today, she would have been tempted and expected to do a livestream or a Reel of her and her sons filling the empty jars. Oh, the views and subscribers a miracle like that would have gotten her! But this wasn't a miracle for everyone to witness. No, this miracle was planned for only the widow and her sons.

God may have miracles planned for you that are only intended for you and your family to see. If He is leading you to shut the door, I hope and pray you'll be obedient. Shut the door and watch the blessings pour out!

Prayer Prompts for Today

~ Is God leading you to do something where "shutting the door" might help you get started on or continue a task? If so, pray over your calling and shut the door.

~ Are you serving in an area where you've gotten distracted by seeking attention? Christians should always place the focus on God, not ourselves. If you find your motives have shifted, pray—ask for God's forgiveness and for Him to realign your thinking and goals.

PERMANENT INK

*This means that anyone who belongs to
Christ has become a new person. The old
life is gone; a new life has begun!*

2 Corinthians 5:17, NLT

"I can't believe I said that!"
"What was I thinking?"
"I can't change or fix what I did."
"They must think I'm awful."

Have you ever made any of these statements? I have. I'm human, and because of that fact, I mess up. We all do. While we're able to keep some blunders private, other mistakes are very publicly known. When this happens, we fear we'll only ever be seen as our worst self.

You are so much more than your worst moment. Please don't let a terrible decision become your identity. We all wish our bad choices were written in pencil so we could erase them, but they're not. They're written in permanent ink. Although we can't erase the ink, we can mark through it. We can scribble through that label and write a new identity next to it. We can change. We can ask forgiveness of God and of those we've wronged. We can make new decisions. We can move on and leave our worst self behind us. Because of what Jesus did on the cross, we can be made new.

If you have a huge mistake in your past, you need to forgive yourself—not forgive and forget (as if that were possible) because memories can help us to not repeat a mistake. They help us learn. But don't give yesterday power over today or tomorrow. Give that power back to God.

Prayer Prompts for Today

~ If you have something in your past that you cannot move on from, pray to God.

Ask Him to forgive you for that past decision and free you from the power of those memories.

~ If you've messed up, ask God's forgiveness. Go to those you've wronged (in person, over the phone, in a letter, etc.) and ask their forgiveness too. Do all you can to try to make things right. Follow God's leading toward becoming a changed person.

18

HATE

*For we are God's handiwork, created in
Christ Jesus to do good works, which God
prepared in advance for us to do.*

Ephesians 2:10, NIV

My eleven-year-old daughter, Madelyn, was eating
breakfast one morning while I was putting dishes
away. She and I were discussing our family's upcoming calendar. We'd been invited to a fun event,

and I was explaining to Madelyn why we wouldn't be able to attend. We couldn't go because the location wasn't safe for Madelyn and my son, Derek, because of their cystic fibrosis.

Madelyn was disappointed—rightfully so. She let out a huge sigh and said, "I hate CF, Mom."

I kept putting away dishes as I said, "I don't."

"You *don't* hate CF? Why?" she asked.

"Because I could never hate anything that's a part of you," I answered.

Silence. She didn't say anything back. So I turned around to look at her. She'd stopped eating. She had a huge smile on her face and tears in her eyes.

"Thank you," she whispered.

Were you or one of your loved ones born with a physical or mental difficulty? It's easy to focus only on what the ailment keeps us from doing. We can fixate so much on it that feelings of hate seep into our thoughts and lives. We can start to hate how God made us. We can resent something about us that we cannot change.

I am a firm believer that God uses every part of who we are to make us into the person He wants us to be. He also uses our difficulties to reach others for Him. Madelyn and Derek witness to and encourage people who have cystic fibrosis in ways that I never could. My children can use their physical weakness as a spiritual strength—a mighty tool for God—and so can you!

Prayer Prompts for Today

~ Were you born with a difficulty that you feel resentment toward? If so, ask God to protect your heart and mind from hate. Ask Him to show you how you can use your situation to reach others for Him.

~ Do you have a loved one who was born with physical or mental disability? Ask God to help your attitude be loving, encouraging, and patient. Pray that He will constantly remind you of the value your loved one has from just being who and how God made them to be.

19

GRACE, NOT GOSSIP

Set a guard over my mouth, LORD;
keep watch over the door of my lips.

Psalm 141:3, NIV

When I was twenty years old, we had a work day at my church. Another lady and I were working together in one of the classrooms. She was about ten years older than me. As we were sorting through some papers, she got a text, read it, and immediately starting sobbing. She kept saying, "I'm sorry! I'm so sorry!" as she cried. I didn't know what to do, so I hugged her. I didn't ask questions. I just held her and patted her back while she sobbed. After a few minutes, she regained her composure and then took a step back so she could look at me.

"My husband is having an affair. He has been for a long time, and . . . I don't know what to do."

At that statement, I started crying with her. She apologized for telling me and asked me to "please, please not tell anyone." I promised her I wouldn't say a word. She told me that she had to go and then started crying again because she was leaving me to finish our project alone. I told her not to worry about it, and she left.

A week later, I was in a hair salon waiting for my turn. I heard one of the hairdressers talking to the lady in her chair. What caught my attention was one of the ladies saying the name of the woman who'd cried with me the week before.

I heard the lady who was having her hair done say, "Well, I saw her yesterday, and she didn't say one word to me. She's been acting so stuck-up lately!"

The hairdresser replied, "Oh, I know! She's been so standoffish and, honestly, just rude lately."

Those two ladies had no idea what that woman was going through. They didn't know that she was barely hanging on by a thread. She needed their grace, not their gossip.

We have no idea what people are going through. We only see what they show us, and that's not always a true representation of what's really happening in their lives. Like that woman, others need our grace, not our gossip.

The same is also true for you. No one really knows everything you're going through—no one except God. He knows. He sees it all. He always understands. He never jumps to conclusions. He always gives grace.

Prayer Prompts for Today

~ Have you ever been met with gossip instead of grace? If so, I am so sorry. Ask God to ease and heal any pain remaining from those memories.

~ Can you think of a time or times when you've given gossip instead of grace? Pray and ask for God's forgiveness. Ask Him how you can remedy your behavior. If you feel Him leading you to apologize to someone, please be obedient.

My Hands

Yes, my soul, find rest in God;
my hope comes from him.

Psalm 62:5, NIV

I was diagnosed with Ehlers-Danlos syndrome just before I turned forty years old. One of my main struggles with the syndrome is that my right hand's fingers constantly come out of their sockets. This . . . is no fun, to say the least. Thankfully, since being diagnosed, I've learned many techniques and tools to help me with my physical issues.

Some days are harder than others. I try to not complain. My typical mantra is, "It is what it is. Complaining won't help." The worst time for my hands so far was in December of 2023. There were three weeks then where I could barely even use my hands—cooking, wrapping gifts, writing, and typing were unbelievably painful.

During that time, I was reading the book *The Princess and the Goblin* by George MacDonald to my daughter. I didn't know much about MacDonald, so I Googled his name, unaware of the blessing I was about to receive. One of the many articles I read about George MacDonald contained this quote:

"We don't have a soul. We are a soul.
We have a body."[2]

As my hands ached, I read that quote. I read it again and again. I mentally changed the words to: "I don't *have* a soul. I *am* a soul. I *have* a body."

At that time, I was mentally struggling over my body. I felt that as I continued to age, my hands would most likely just worsen. I was overwhelmed with scenarios of how my hands would always be a problem for me.

MacDonald's quote reminded me that my situation—my body, my hands—is temporary. My body won't last forever, but my soul will. Before my struggles with my hands, my thoughts of Heaven were mainly about how I'll be with Jesus, I'll see loved ones who've gone on before me, and there will be no sin. Now, I also think about how there will be no more pain. In Heaven, my hands will be perfect!

Is your body failing you? Do you, too, have days when you're overcome with your physical limitations? Maybe MacDonald's quote can bring you comfort as well. You are not your aching body. You are your strong, indestructible soul—a soul that will live forever. If you are a child of God, one day we'll be together in Heaven, and when I see you there, I know I'll clap my perfect hands together in joy!

Prayer Prompts for Today

~ If you are physically struggling, pray for God to give you relief, hope, strength, and the wisdom to make choices that help your body.

~ Pray for your loved ones who have physical issues and limitations.

~ Take time to thank God for who He is and for His promises of Heaven.

HUMILITY

When pride comes, then comes disgrace,
but with humility comes wisdom.

Proverbs 11:2, NIV

Humility is the fear of the LORD;
its wages are riches and honor and life.

Proverbs 22:4, NIV

*For all those who exalt themselves will
be humbled, and those who humble
themselves will be exalted.*

Luke 14:11, NIV

*Live in harmony with one another. Do not be
proud; instead, associate with the humble.
Do not be wise in your own estimation.*

Romans 12:16, CSB

*Do nothing out of selfish ambition or vain
conceit. Rather, in humility value others above
yourselves, not looking to your own interests
but each of you to the interests of the others.*

Philippians 2:3-4, NIV

*Therefore, as God's chosen people, holy and
dearly loved, clothe yourselves with compassion,
kindness, humility, gentleness and patience.*

Colossians 3:12, NIV

*But he gives us more grace. That is why
Scripture says: "God opposes the proud
but shows favor to the humble."*

James 4:6, NIV

Humble yourselves before the LORD,
and he will lift you up.

James 4:10, NIV

As you can see, I struggled with choosing the key passage for this devotion because the Bible has *so* much to teach us about being humble. Humility pleases God.

The opposite of humble is proud. Being prideful is dangerous. Proverbs 16:18 (NKJV) tells us, "Pride goes before destruction, and a haughty spirit before a fall." Besides being dangerous, being filled with pride is just downright unlikable. Arrogance is off-putting. If you are a Christian, your witness will suffer if it is clothed in arrogance.

One of the biggest wake-up calls God uses to snap us out of our arrogance is perspective. Most of us have been there—where we thought we knew exactly how something would be, and God gives us a healthy dose of perspective. We then realize that we don't know as much as we previously thought.

We must be careful to not be arrogantly humble—which I know sounds like an oxymoron. We shouldn't be proud of our humility. We need to hold our actions and motives accountable and try to keep them pure. If we're only acting humble so our humility can be seen, then we're just showing off.

So, what does true humility look like? Well, we have the ultimate example of humility in our Savior, Jesus Christ. He gave up His glory to become human. He lowered Himself for us.

In your relationships with one another, have the same mindset as Christ Jesus: Who, being in very nature God, did not consider equality with God something to be used to his own advantage; rather, he made himself nothing by taking the very nature of a servant, being made in human likeness. And being found in appearance as a man, he humbled himself by becoming obedient to death—even death on a cross!

Philippians 2:5-8, NIV

PRAYER PROMPTS FOR TODAY

~ Ask God to show you if there is arrogance in your life. If He reveals something to you, ask for His forgiveness and help. Pray that He will transform that pride into humility.

Grow Up

*Brothers and sisters, stop thinking like
children. In regard to evil be infants,
but in your thinking be adults.*

1 Corinthians 14:20, NIV

I believe one of the best opening lines was written
by J. M. Barrie in his book *Peter Pan*.

"All children, except one, grow up."[3]

I just love this opening! It is so well written. It's concise. It makes you wonder who the "one" is and why he/she doesn't have to grow up. Merriam-Webster defines the phrase *grow up* as "to grow toward or arrive at full stature or physical or mental maturity: to progress from childhood toward adulthood; to become an adult; to stop thinking or behaving in a childish way."[4]

Barrie was correct that all children do grow up physically to be adults, but unfortunately, not all adults "grow up." An accumulation of years and experiences does not ensure maturity.

Let's look at some signs of growing up and maturing. One is being able to make yourself do what needs to be done now, whether you want to or not, because you see how your actions affect your future and the futures of your loved ones. In other words, making yourself do what you don't feel like doing. There are so many examples for this: exercising, saving, telling the truth, studying, practicing, cleaning . . . I could go on and on.

Another sign of maturity is thinking before you speak—not just rattling off right when the emotion hits you. This symptom of maturity shows an understanding of words having power and that they cannot be taken back. James 1:19-20 (NLT) tells us, "Understand this, my dear brothers and sisters: You must all be quick to listen, slow to speak, and slow to get angry. Human anger does not produce the righteousness God desires."

Another indication of growing up is not depending on others to tell you what you should do. Mature individuals take care of their responsibilities without needing to be prompted. Also, looking at our responsibilities and tasks as blessings and not burdens helps our attitudes. We must remember that being physically and mentally able to handle our responsibilities is a blessing.

Another badge of maturing is being able to see the value of the people in our lives. When we are mindful of how much our loved ones add to our lives, we live with a thankful attitude. We treat others with respect, we appreciate them, we value them. God wants us to see value in *all* people—those we get along with and those we don't. Spiritual maturity allows us to see every individual as a person who God created and loves dearly.

It's easy to see areas in other people's lives where they need to "grow up," but it's much more difficult to see those places in our own lives. Habits and intentions can sometimes cloud our self-view. Please take time to intentionally evaluate your actions over the next couple weeks. If you notice moments where you act a bit like Peter Pan, that's good! Noticing where you need to change and grow is great! Now that you've seen those areas, you're ready to really grow.

Prayer Prompts for Today

~ Did any of these signs of maturity step on your toes? If so, pray about those areas in your life. Ask God to help you grow and mature in how you handle situations.

It Only Takes Seconds

Blessed are those who mourn,
for they shall be comforted.

Matthew 5:4, NKJV

My dad passed away on January 18, 2024. He battled Lewy body dementia for years. Since we had time to plan for Dad's death, I thought I knew how I'd react and feel. What I've learned since then is that you never really know how you'll feel or act until things actually happen.

One reaction I had when my dad passed that surprised me was the need I felt for comfort from others. I've always loved to celebrate with others, but I prefer to grieve alone. When my dad died, I was surprised by how much it meant to me for people to reach out. My family was truly taken care of and blessed when Dad left us. The food, care packages, flowers, cards, messages, visits, posts, Christmas ornaments, and calls soothed our souls. We felt unbelievably loved.

During my immediate time of grieving, I was surprised by how much I didn't care *what* anyone did, I just really cared that they *did* something. *Anything.* Since I first created my Facebook account twenty years ago, I have honestly never looked to see who all clicked the like, love, or care buttons on my posts. But when my dad died, I did. I don't know why. I would check to see who clicked the emotions on my posts, my sister's posts, and my mom's posts about Dad. I clicked on my mom and dad's church post about his funeral. I read every single comment anywhere on Facebook about my dad's passing. If anyone did anything—even just clicking the care emoji on a post—I felt comfort. It felt like that person taking two seconds to click an emotion was them wanting to let us know that they really did care.

I have a new perspective on death and grieving now. When I see a post letting others know about a loved one's passing, I always click the care button. Because I know now that even a tiny act like that can bring comfort to a hurting heart. Let's always take the time—even if it's just two seconds—to let others know that we care.

PRAYER PROMPTS FOR TODAY

~ Pray for the people in your life who are grieving.

~ Reach out to them and let them know you care. That may look like you sending them a casserole or a card, or it may be as simple as clicking the care button on Facebook.

THE BIG PICTURE

Don't look out only for your own interests,
but take an interest in others, too.

Philippians 2:4, NLT

I graduated in 2006 with a bachelor of fine arts in photography. I was in college at a very interesting time in photography's history. My first two years were film and darkroom photography. My last two years were digital photography.

With digital photography, photos can be enlarged on a computer screen to where you're looking at individual pixels. These pixels look like small squares of color. When you zoom out, you can see that all the combined pixels make up the image.

When we focus on only one pixel of a photo, we can't see the big picture. Likewise, when I focus only on myself in situations, I can't see the big picture. The big picture includes other people, their feelings, and their circumstances. When I focus only on myself, I only see *my* feelings, *my* goals, and *my* circumstances. Focusing on myself encourages me to be self-absorbed and self-centered, whereas focusing on others encourages me to be thoughtful and compassionate.

If you're like me, the easiest times to be self-focused are when situations and circumstances don't go the way I think they should. In these moments, we must intentionally keep the big picture in sight. Focusing on others allows us to see where patience, understanding, and grace are needed. The more we focus on others, the more that practice becomes a habit. Practicing what we choose to focus on and how we view situations allows us to see the beautiful picture that God is creating.

If you have a tendency to focus mostly on yourself, then it's time to zoom out and refocus on the big picture.

Prayer Prompts for Today

~ Ask God to keep you ever mindful of the big picture in situations.

~ Pray that your focus will be where it should be. Ask God to help you be eager and ready to give grace to others.

~ Are you reminded of a time when you focused on yourself and shouldn't have? Ask God for forgiveness. If He leads you to ask someone else for their forgiveness too, please be obedient.

THE REAL YOU

*You have searched me, LORD, and you
know me. You know when I sit and when
I rise; you perceive my thoughts from afar.
You discern my going out and my lying
down; you are familiar with all my ways.
Before a word is on my tongue you,
LORD, know it completely.*

Psalm 139:1-4, NIV

My sister used to play the keyboard on the worship team of a very large church. Years ago, I spent a weekend with her, and I accompanied her to the worship team's preservice practice. I sat in the sanctuary and watched as the band, praise team, and tech team ran through the songs.

A young man on the praise team was going to pray during the service at the end of one of the songs. The music director told the band to play some of their last song again so the young man could practice praying while the band accompanied him. They did, and the young man prayed a beautiful, heartfelt prayer.

What happened next shocked me. The music director looked at the young man and said into the mic, "Okay, that was good, but I'm gonna need you to pray with a lot more energy and speak higher."

The young man looked confused and asked, "You want me to pray louder?"

"No," the music director answered. "I need your voice to have a higher pitch when you pray. You need to sound higher. Your speaking voice is too low."

I thought, *I'm sorry, what? Did he really just tell his praise team member to change his voice when he* prays?

Yes. Yes, he did, and during the service, the praise team member prayed with more energy and a higher tone. To me, the prayer felt performed. I could be wrong. My feelings and thoughts were probably swayed by me being privy to their "prayer rehearsal." All I know is that I didn't like the music director telling someone to change their natural speaking voice when they prayed.

I understand that when we lead others in public prayer, we do need to make sure our voices are loud, clear, and easily understandable. But we need to use *our* voices. We shouldn't try to sound like someone else.

Since that experience, I've heard a similar "prayer voice" from others leading prayer—a voice that sounds higher than the person's natural voice, and their words are connected together in a "sing-song" sound. There's a similar softly shouted urgency in the voices. Now, please understand what I am *not* saying—I am not judging the words of anyone's prayer or their hearts. It's solely the uniform sound that concerns me. I fear this "prayer voice" is being taught in some places, and that makes me sad. I don't want anyone telling you, me, or my kids that our natural God-given voices aren't what we should use when speaking to the Lord.

God wants the unique, different-sounding you. You don't need to try to sound like someone else. I hope this devotion helps us be more aware of what we're presenting to God. He wants the real us—the *real* you. He gave you the voice you have, your mannerisms, and your unique sound. God loves your voice just as it is.

Prayer Prompts for Today

~ Conversation is such an important part in every relationship. God wants a relationship with you and real conversation with you. When praying, do you typically repeat certain phrases to Him? Do you try to sound very formal? Do you rush through your prayer because you don't feel comfortable figuring out what to say? The next time you pray, focus on talking to God—really talking. No one else in the world will have the exact same conversations with God as you do, and that's precisely how it should be!

TODAY

*Do not boast about tomorrow, for you
do not know what a day may bring.*

Proverbs 27:1, ESV

Benjamin Franklin wrote, "Never leave till tomorrow that which you can do today."[5] We all make future plans, but in doing so, we must always remember that tomorrow is guaranteed to no one. So, let's seize today!

TODAY

Song written by Amanda Allen (my sister)

I look back on the years that I wasted on nothing
Just breathing to breathe
Now I'm older
I want to be remembered for something
Something bigger than me
I've been caught up in myself
Backing into corners
Bumping into walls
Now I want to take the books off of the shelf
and read them all
Today

Call my parents just for the good conversation
Maybe some advice
Hold a baby and suddenly get the sensation
that someday this might be nice
I've been running from myself
Dodging every bullet
Hiding from the pain
Now I want to put the umbrella on the shelf
and feel the rain
Today

There's no more time to borrow
No more bargains to make
The future isn't tomorrow
It all starts today

I've been looking at myself
Asking for the answers
Learning from mistakes
There's a mirror on the shelf
I won't look away

PRAYER PROMPTS FOR TODAY

~ Is there something you feel God has been calling you to do, but you've been putting it off? Ask Him to give you the wisdom and energy to start the project today! If God is leading you to do the task, He will bless your efforts.

Scan the QR code to hear
my sister singing "Today."

I WAS MANIPULATING!

*Do nothing out of selfish ambition
or vain conceit. Rather, in humility
value others above yourselves . . .*

Philippians 2:3, NIV

Manipulation has so many tactics in its arsenal: playing the victim, guilt-tripping, excessive flattery, gaslighting, shifting blame, making threats, using charm offensively, exploiting vulnerabilities, controlling behavior, lying, and creating a sense of dependency. If you use any of these tactics on someone in your life, you are manipulating them. If you word things or act in a certain way to get what you want, you are being manipulative. You are trying to control another person's actions or emotions, and God cannot bless that.

Manipulation is wrong. Even when we're trying to get someone we love to do something good, it is still wrong to manipulate them. We can bring wisdom to the table, but we can't make anyone eat. We must allow the adults in our lives to make their own choices. We have to let go of control, give situations and people to God, and realize that we cannot make anyone do anything.

One of the strongest manipulation tactics I see women in particular using is guilt. Ladies, we *have* to stop this. Guilt-tripping puts such a strain on relationships and causes more stress than I can even begin to say. I've witnessed this form of manipulation poured out on many adult children by their mothers, and let me tell you, the quickest way to make a child not want to be with or talk to their mother is to constantly guilt them into doing things, saying things, and being places. Mothers, if you want a strong, close relationship with your adult children, you cannot guilt them into doing what you want.

I have discussed the subject of manipulation with my kids many times. Why? Because I want them to grow into adults who can hopefully spot its tactics a mile away. I do not want my daughter or son to be manipulated *by* others or be manipulative *to* others.

When my son was nine, we were about to pass our town's Chick-fil-A. Derek said, "Can we please have diet lemonades?"

I said, "No, not today."

Derek said, "Oh, okay." Then ten seconds later, he said, "Whew, it's really hot today. I sure wish I had a cold drink. A lemonade would have been great, but you said no. And we've been really good lately too, but—" Then he gasped and said, "Mom! I was manipulating!"

I just laughed and said, "Ding! Ding! Ding! Good job catching that, bud."

Being manipulative can become a habit, and you may not even realize when you're doing it. So, listen to yourself, watch your actions, and check your motives. You, too, may gasp and say, "I was manipulating!"

PRAYER PROMPTS FOR TODAY

~ Do you word things or act in a certain way to get what you want? If you do, pray for God to help you stop being manipulative. He may press upon your heart the need to apologize to people in your life. Please be obedient.

~ Do you struggle with a manipulative relationship? If so, pray that God will open their eyes and convict their hearts. Ask God to show you how He'd have you handle that relationship.

28

COMMAS, NOT PERIODS.

Therefore, if anyone is in Christ, he is a new creation; old things have passed away; behold, all things have become new.

2 Corinthians 5:17, NKJV

I've worked with teenagers for years—in music lessons, plays, youth groups, and choirs. My memories of those interactions are mostly wonderful. Occasionally, I work with a difficult teen. I try to be very understanding and patient with kids—they're still learning and adjusting to new hormones and bodies, and many come from troubled home situations.

However, my patience quickly wears thin from disrespect and arrogance, but it's a certain type of arrogance that really gets to me. Some teens may come across as "braggy," but that behavior often stems from insecurities. My patience stays intact with this type of arrogance. The arrogance that chips away at my patience is the kind that truly thinks they know everything and are better than others.

There was one teen who was super arrogant (to me and her classmates) and extremely disrespectful. I tried to be kind and a good, supportive influence on her, but to be honest, I did not enjoy being around this young lady at all.

Many years after I worked with her, I saw her again at an event. Do you know the first word that came to my mind when I saw her?

Brat.

Yep, I saw her years later when she was married, a mom, an employee . . . She'd gained life perspective, she'd grown up, and the only way I still saw her was as a brat.

Friends, that is *not* okay.

Sometimes, we do not allow people to change. We don't allow them to grow. We can easily put a period after a description where God puts a comma.

It bothers me to wonder: What if I'd met Paul after he changed from being Saul (Acts 9:1-31)? I hope and pray I would not have labeled him as only a murderer.

God is the instigator and facilitator of change. God *changes* people. God looked at Paul and, yes, acknowledged his past—he *was* a murderer of Christ's followers—but God then put a comma and described Paul after he changed. God saw Paul as a new creation.

God does that for us too. He puts a comma where, unfortunately, some people may have put a period. Christians should truly believe that God can change people. He can change a period into a comma.

PRAYER PROMPTS FOR TODAY

~ If you see a person trying to change, pray for them. Cheer them on!

~ Ask God to help you see people as they currently are—not just as they used to be. Ask Him to help you put commas instead of periods.

29

LEAD US NOT INTO TEMPTATION

After this manner therefore pray ye:
Our Father which art in heaven, Hallowed
be thy name. Thy kingdom come, Thy will be
done in earth, as it is in heaven. Give us this
day our daily bread. And forgive us our
debts, as we forgive our debtors. And lead
us not into temptation, but deliver us from
evil: For thine is the kingdom, and the
power, and the glory, for ever. Amen.

Matthew 6:9-13, KJV

I grew up reciting the Lord's Prayer in church. In my younger years, I honestly never thought much about the words or what they meant. I was just focused on making sure I quoted the prayer correctly.

A few years ago, I read the prayer and actually paid attention to the words. I felt fine until I got to verse 13.

And lead us not into temptation,
but deliver us from evil . . .

I felt confused and, honestly, angry. I always thought of God as my heavenly Father, and this verse felt like it was telling me that He would lead me into temptation—*lead* me into harm. It felt wrong to me that in our model prayer, we're being taught that we have to ask our *Father* to please not lead us into temptation. Shouldn't He be protecting us from temptations?

At the time, my children were six and four years old. I couldn't process or fathom the thought of me, as their parent, knowingly and willingly *leading* them into temptations, leading them into situations or habits that could harm them.

This planted a feeling of distrust and resentment in my heart toward my Lord and Savior. Unfortunately, I never asked my pastor or someone wiser than me for council. Why is it that many of us so often won't admit when we're confused or upset about religious topics? For me, the answer was I didn't want to spread my confusion or anger with others or have anyone think badly of my weak faith.

A few months ago, one of my dear friends, Allison, started a Wednesday night women's class at our church. I knew the class would be wonderful, but on the first night, I almost didn't go. It had been a *long* day, and I desperately wanted to just get into my pajamas, lie in my favorite chair, and watch a cooking show. But I went, and I'm so very thankful I did.

I can't remember what that first night's lesson was on, but I will never forget a portion of what Allison taught our class. She told us that God will lovingly reveal what tempts us. She said that we should want Him to show us our temptations because if we don't learn what they are, we won't know where we're vulnerable or how evil could potentially draw us in.

Honestly, after she shared that with us, my ears turned off. I don't remember listening or being mentally "there" for the remainder of the class. I was so full of relief and appreciation. I felt like God had given Allison those thoughts to share with our group just for me. I finally felt peace about the Lord's Prayer.

A few weeks ago, I shared all of this with Allison. She pointed me to this passage:

Let no one say when he is tempted,
"I am tempted by God"; for God cannot be
tempted by evil, nor does He Himself tempt
anyone. But each one is tempted when he
is drawn away by his own desires and
enticed. Then, when desire has conceived,
it gives birth to sin; and sin, when it is
full-grown, brings forth death.

James 1:13-15, NKJV

God does not want us to be overwhelmed by our temptations to the degree that we're captured by evil and sin. God will never entice us to sin. But when we are tempted, He is our present help and deliverer.

Allison also encouraged me to research the Lord's Prayer. She said that when scripture was translated from Greek, there were sometimes multiple English words that the translators could choose from. So I did, and wouldn't you know it, she was right! The Greek word for temptation can also mean testing. Finding that out brought me even more peace.

God *does* protect us, but in His perfect wisdom, He decides when our faith, our lives, and our beliefs need to be tested. He may reveal what tempts you to show you where you're vulnerable. Why? Because our loving Father is protecting you.

PRAYER PROMPTS FOR TODAY

~ Do you have a spiritual concern that troubles you? Maybe something that you don't understand? Have you talked to your pastor, researched it more, or prayed about it? You should! Remember, it isn't weakness to ask for help when you don't understand something—it's wisdom.

~ Read the Lord's Prayer aloud. Thank God for how He protects you.

~ Ask Him to reveal what tempts you so you'll be more aware of how evil may try to pull you in.

~ If you do realize a temptation, give it to God. Pray for His help and guidance. Also, ask trusted confidants to pray for you in this area and keep you accountable.

MIND YOUR OWN BUSINESS

. . . and to make it your ambition to lead a quiet life: You should mind your own business and work with your hands, just as we told you . . .

1 Thessalonians 4:11, NIV

And there we have it, friends—minding our own business is spiritual maturity. I find the frankness in 1 Thessalonians 4:11 very refreshing. Most of us would love to live a quiet, less stressful life, but social media can make minding our own business a bit difficult. All the photos and posts we come across can be fodder for gossip, insecurities, and envy.

1 Thessalonians 4:11 encourages people to "work with your hands." What does that mean, and why does that statement follow "mind your own business"? How is working with your hands and minding your own business related to living a quiet life?

One of the best ways for us to mind our own business is to not be lazy. When we're busy, when we're working, we don't have time to scroll on social media for hours. Being productive can protect us from all that online "noise" and help us lead a quiet life.

Prayer Prompts for Today

~ Do you spend too much time on social media? If yes, pray for God to help you set and adhere to time limits.

~ Is online "noise" drowning out your quiet life? Pray about implementing some healthy online boundaries.

31

It Just Takes One Friend

Do to others as you would have them do to you.

Luke 6:31, NIV

When I was growing up, I went to GA (Girls in Action) Camp. This was a weeklong camp during the summer. We stayed in cabins, went on hikes, had quiet times, learned about missions, met missionaries, made crafts, sang silly songs . . . It was great! Well, the first year I went *wasn't* great.

In fact, it was quite miserable—so much so that I almost didn't go back the following year. But I did, and that second summer was wonderful!

Why? What changed? It was the same camp both years—same location, same activities. What wasn't the same was *who* I was at camp with. That first year, a girl from my community also went to GA Camp. We were put into the same cabin, and . . . she was very mean to me. This confused me at the time because she didn't even know me. The most we'd ever spoken to each other or been together before camp was on the drive *to* camp (we carpooled). The car ride there was fine, but when we arrived, she changed.

I couldn't understand why she became so mean or why she rallied the other girls in our cabin to not like me. As an adult, I can now look back and see why. She was a kid who didn't want others to make fun of her, not like her, or leave her out. Like all kids, she wanted to fit in. So, she selected someone to be "the girl" so that it wouldn't be her, and unfortunately, she chose me.

As a result, my first year of camp was not fun. I couldn't fully enjoy any of the awesome activities because of the dynamic this girl had created in our cabin. I remember feeling left out and just wanting to go home.

The next year, my best friend wanted to go to GA Camp. She was a year younger than me, and this was her first year to be old enough to go. She asked if I'd go with her, and my immediate response was, "No! I hated it!" But after a bit of convincing, she talked me into going back, and I had the *best* time—so much so that we went back again together the following year too.

I've seen my GA Camp experience play out again and again with people in my adult life.

- Two people go to the same party—one is having fun getting to know new people while the other is miserable and feels invisible.
- Two ladies go to the same women's conference—one tells me she loved it and had the best time, the other tells me that it was boring and awful.
- Two teens in their youth group—one loves going to Sunday school and feels so close to fellow students while the other feels left out and sits alone.

Events, locations, decorations, and activities can't make people love an experience or have great memories. What can? Positive interactions with people—that's what impacts people's enjoyment the most. In fact, having just one friend with you can make a not-so-great event be one that you thoroughly enjoyed. We all want to have at least one friend like that—someone who makes "camp" fun for us. We must also want to be that type of friend for others too.

Prayer Prompts for Today

~ Think of a time when someone made an event or experience so much more enjoyable for you. Thank God for that person.

~ Pray and ask God to help you look for opportunities where you can improve someone else's experience.

PAY ON TIME

*Let no debt remain outstanding, except
the continuing debt to love one another, for
whoever loves others has fulfilled the law.*

Romans 13:8, NIV

My mother has taught music lessons for over fifty
years. My sister and I also taught music for many
years. All three of us would agree that we love
everything about teaching music except for one

thing: having to "chase" people to pay for their lessons. Some parents would just drop their kids off repeatedly, knowing they hadn't paid for their child's music lessons in weeks.

Why do people accept services and then not pay? Let's look at three possible reasons why. The first is the most upsetting: Some people knowingly try to take advantage of others. They want to get the most they can for free. This behavior is, of course, not Christlike and goes against God's teaching. In Leviticus 19:11, NKJV, God tells us: "You shall not steal, nor deal falsely, nor lie to one another."

The second reason may be carelessness. Some people aren't intentionally trying to cause problems or be rude, they're just busy and don't realize how inconsiderate their behavior is. While it's good that their actions aren't filled with malice, they're still doing wrong and causing harm. Remember, we judge ourselves by our intentions, but others judge us by our actions.

The last reason is the one I believe is mostly to blame. I think many people subconsciously behave like everyone else's financial situations are similar to theirs. If they don't have to worry about money, they don't know what it feels like. Or maybe they've forgotten that others do deal with money concerns. They fail to realize that the person they're interacting with may live paycheck to paycheck.

Many years ago, my sister, Amanda, taught lessons for a wealthy family. They definitely had the money to pay for their children's piano lessons. But so many times, the mom would drop her kids off for lessons without a tuition check for her kids to give to Manda. My sister would be forced to message the mother and ask about payment, which is awkward! The mom would nonchalantly say, "Oh! I'm so sorry. I forgot again. I'll send it next week." It was no big deal . . . to the mom. But it was a *huge* deal for my sister. Manda, like all of us, had bills due and was frequently stressed when people did not pay her the money she'd earned—on time.

Unfortunately, some people seem to be unfazed about owing others money. Ladies, let's make sure that sentence doesn't describe us. Let's be women who do right by and take care of the people we interact with.

PRAYER PROMPTS FOR TODAY

~ Did someone's name come to your mind as you read this devotion? Do you need to make things right with them and apologize for any stress you may have caused?

~ Do you have a habit of not paying people on time? Ask God to help you change that behavior.

33

LISTENING

*My dear brothers and sisters, take note of this:
Everyone should be quick to listen, slow to
speak and slow to become angry . . .*

James 1:19, NIV

I am a better listener today than I used to be. When
I was younger, I had the tendency to "listen" only
while waiting to talk next. When others would
speak, I'd so often try to appear to be listening while

I was actually busy thinking about what I was about to say when they finished talking.

Listening—true listening, where you actually hear and remember what a person says—is a skill and habit that I have had to learn. I still struggle at times, but I'm slowly improving.

Are you a chatterbox, like me? Conversation is how I feel close to others. But I have to watch myself on not monopolizing the conversation. When I first realized that I wasn't a very good listener, I had to almost bite my tongue at times so that I wouldn't interrupt the other person.

Over the years, I've realized the importance of listening—and not only listening, but the importance of others feeling heard. We all want to be heard, and we all want what we've said to be remembered.

In James 1:19, the Bible tells us to be quick to listen and slow to speak. The wisdom in that verse is huge! For many of us, our natural tendency is the opposite—we're *slow* to listen and *quick* to speak. This causes us to also be slow to remember and quick to react, slow to receive instruction and quick to say the wrong thing, slow to understand and quick to go off on a tangent. I can't tell you how many times I've thought, *Oh, I wish I hadn't said that!* We save ourselves so much stress, embarrassment, and regret when we focus more on listening than speaking.

Prayer Prompts for Today

~ Are you a good listener? If you, too, struggle, pray and ask God to help you improve your listening skills.

~ Do you remember what your loved ones tell you? Special dates, upcoming events, concerns . . . Do you remember to pray about what they've shared? Do you check on them? Spend some time praying for your loved ones and the details they've shared with you.

~ At your next available opportunity, contact a loved one and check in on them. Let them know you've been praying for them and their situation.

34

WHAT IF?

*Do not neglect to do good and to share what you
have, for such sacrifices are pleasing to God.*

Hebrews 13:16, ESV

In 2019, my sister and I were hired to lead the music for a women's conference. The event was held at
a church in the town we grew up in, so we knew
almost every woman attending. While leading the
first song, I noticed a young lady in the far-right

section of the sanctuary. I spotted her for a couple of reasons: one, I didn't recognize her, and two, she was alone. Most, if not all, of the women in the congregation were standing next to other ladies, but this woman had no one on either side of her.

Our first song set ended, and the conference continued. I didn't think more about the woman I'd seen earlier until we all went to the church's fellowship hall for lunch. As I mentioned, this conference was at a church in our childhood hometown. My mom and aunt were in attendance, along with many other of my relatives and close friends.

I was standing in line waiting to receive a delicious Nancy's Lunchbox chicken salad sandwich. I looked to my right and saw my mom, aunt, and sister sitting at a table. Once I got my food, I turned to head their way but stopped. The fellowship hall's tables were all filled with ladies . . . all except for the table right in front of me. At this table, there sat only one woman—the lady I'd seen during the opening song.

I clearly felt God tell me to sit down next to her. I'm ashamed now, even as I write this, to tell you that I didn't do it. I didn't obey Him. Why? I wanted to sit with my family. I looked over at the ladies still in line for food and thought that surely someone would end up sitting with her.

I spoke to her as I passed her table. I said, "You have the most gorgeous hair. (Which she did.) I have total hair envy right now!"

She smiled and replied, "Thank you."

I felt better. I'd spoken to her and been kind, so it was probably okay that I went to sit with my family and friends. Besides, surely someone still in the line would end up sitting with her.

After the meal, all the women went to various classes. Once those classes ended, everyone returned to the sanctuary for the closing service. I took my place onstage for the last worship set, and the lady who'd been sitting alone came to my mind. I glanced where she'd sat earlier. The seat was empty. As the music started, my eyes frantically searched every seat in the sanctuary. She wasn't there.

Why did she leave? Maybe she had somewhere to be and had planned on leaving early. Or maybe something urgent happened and she had to go. Or maybe . . . maybe she was lonely and neglected. I'd assumed that other ladies would probably sit with her at lunch, but did they? What if they hadn't? Maybe she felt uncomfortable and embarrassed that no one was sitting with her, so she left.

This conference will forever be a painful memory for me. I disobeyed God.

I know He told me to sit with her, but I didn't want to. Don't get me wrong, I really do love meeting new people. But that Saturday, I was surrounded by my family and friends. I wanted to sit with them. I was enjoying familiarity and fellowship, enjoying it so much that I apparently forgot to share it!

Would she have stayed if I'd sat with her? I'll never know, but that question still bothers me to this day. What I do know is that I missed out on opportunities and blessings that day. Most likely, I would have made a new friend. I could have made someone feel included and wanted. The biggest question that truly eats away at me is: What if she had stayed at the conference and accepted Christ? I'll never know.

PRAYER PROMPTS FOR TODAY

~ Can you remember a time when God told you to do something but you didn't obey? If so, ask Him to forgive you.

~ What keeps you at times from following God's leading?

WITH FRIENDS LIKE THESE . . .

Trust in the LORD with all your heart
and lean not on your own understanding;
in all your ways submit to him, and he
will make your paths straight.

Proverbs 3:5-6, NIV

A lady shared at our Wednesday night women's Bible study class that she felt God leading her to pull away from a friendship. She told us that her friend had been "jokingly" putting her down for a while—making jokes about her weight, intelligence, and appearance. With tears in her eyes, she told us how much those comments hurt her. She said, "I don't need a friend to treat me like that."

After the lady shared, an elderly woman told our class that she had painfully ended a friendship years ago because she realized the relationship was bad for her marriage. Her friend would constantly say things to her like, "When is your husband going to move you out of that shoebox and into a *real* house? When is he going to get a better job? Your husband doesn't let you spend enough money," and so on.

She told us that eventually, her friend's comments poisoned her thinking. She began complaining to her husband constantly about how she deserved more from him. She said that after three years of this, she finally realized that her friend was harming her thoughts, behavior, and marriage.

She shared that when God revealed that to her, she went to her husband and apologized. She said he broke down crying and said, "It felt like all you could do was put me down and that I could never do things good enough for you." After hearing that, she immediately ended her friendship.

She closed her eyes and told us, "It was so hard to do." Then she smiled, and with tears in her eyes, she told our class, "But a month after I ended that friendship, my husband and I were laughing and spending time together like the two bestest friends that have ever been! God blessed our marriage."

Walking away from a friendship can be very difficult, even when you know the friendship is un-healthy. You may worry that you'll be lonely without them. You may feel guilty because you see how much the other woman needs you. You may feel mean, like you're abandoning them, but these are never reasons to stay in relationships that are harmful to you.

Do not make friends with a hot-tempered person, do not associate with one easily angered, or you may learn their ways and get yourself ensnared.

Proverbs 22:24-25, NIV

Look also at how the New Living Translation words this verse:

Don't befriend angry people or associate with hot-tempered people, or you will learn to be like them and endanger your soul.

Proverbs 22:24-25, NLT

If God is leading you to walk away from an unhealthy friendship, He will supply you with the strength to do it. He will give you the wisdom to know how and when to end the relationship. He will bless you for being obedient.

Endings can feel sad, but I love how Fred Rogers viewed them:

"Often when you think you're at the end
of something, you're at the beginning
of something else."[6]

And that "something else" could be the start of a beautiful new friendship!

Prayer Prompts for Today

~ Do you have an unhealthy friendship? If you do, ask God how He wants you to handle the relationship.

~ If you feel Him leading you to end the friendship, pray for God to give you peace about that decision.

~ Ask God to show you what to do, and pray for His strength to help you obey.

~ Pray for your former friend. Not having a future with someone doesn't mean that you can't still pray for and love them.

TIME

For where your treasure is,
there your heart will be also.

Matthew 6:21, ESV

Where you spend your money—your treasure—
shows what's important to you. This statement is
also true for how you spend your time. The older I
get, I frequently view time as more valuable than
money. People with declining health or on their

deathbeds don't typically wish they had more money; they wish they had more time. Time is such a precious treasure—time spent in God's Word, time spent with family, time spent serving, time spent improving health, time spent practicing, learning, and growing.

Let's take a moment now and evaluate how we're spending our time—how we're investing this treasure. Think about the past few days and honestly answer the following questions.

- How much time did you spend praying?

- How much time did you spend on social media?

- How much time did you spend reading the Bible?

- How much time did you spend watching TV?

- How much time did you spend with loved ones?

- How much time did you spend shopping?

- How much time did you spend on improving your health?

- How much time did you spend gaming?

- How much time did you spend practicing a talent?

None of the activities in these questions are bad. We all need downtime to unwind and relax. The questions are only to show you how you are balancing time. Do you feel good about how you spent your time? Are you pleased with how you invested this treasure?

In 1693, William Penn wrote, "Time is what we want most, but what we use worst."[7] Time passes so quickly. If we don't consciously evaluate how we're spending it and make needed adjustments, we quickly find William Penn's words to be true.

PRAYER PROMPTS FOR TODAY

~ Pray for God to help you manage your time responsibly. Ask Him to give you wisdom when choosing which activities deserve your time.

~ If you need to adjust your habits, ask God to help you commit to and apply the needed changes. You may want to ask a close relative or friend to be your accountability partner.

ACTORS IN THE CHURCH

*Rescue me, LORD, from evildoers; protect
me from the violent, who devise evil plans in
their hearts and stir up war every day.
They make their tongues as sharp as a
serpent's; the poison of vipers is on their lips.
Keep me safe, LORD, from the hands of the
wicked; protect me from the violent, who
devise ways to trip my feet. The arrogant
have hidden a snare for me; they have
spread out the cords of their net and have*

set traps for me along my path. I say to the
LORD, "You are my God." Hear, LORD,
my cry for mercy.

Psalm 140:1-6, NIV

I was born in 1983, and I've gone to church my
entire life. My parents were evangelists, so we trav-
eled to over forty churches every year for the first
fourteen years of my life. My dad became a pastor
when I was fifteen. As an adult, I have worked at
three churches, the last being on staff for almost a
decade. I'm sharing all of that to explain that I
know a lot about this subject. I have my receipts.

I love God. I love the church (the people), and I
love churches (the buildings, businesses). But I will
say this boldly and with every fiber of my being: We
do *not* know everything about the people we go to
church with. We only know what we see and what
we're told. You can go to church with people for fifty
years and still not know the *real* them. Now, let's be
clear—no one is perfect. If churches were only for
perfect people who had their lives together and
never did anything wrong, then all church buildings
would be empty.

What I want to discuss in this devotion is
"actors" in churches. I've had experiences with
people who act one way in church and then act
completely the opposite in their homes. One of the

many heartbreaking parts in those situations is that their families are forced to maintain the secret. The family members are expected to keep the charade going and make sure that person's perfect facade remains intact. The family is punished if they don't.

When I worked full time in the church, there were numerous times over the years where ladies would schedule meetings with me. When we'd meet, the ladies would pour their hearts and pain out, and here's what I learned:

Many of these ladies were mentally, emotionally, sexually, and/or physically abused as children by a parent. Their abusive parent had been (and often still was) very active in church. These parents were pros at acting one way in public and then transforming into monsters when they got home.

Most of these abused ladies now had children of their own. Many of them decided that in order to protect their sanity and their kids' safety, they would not allow their children to be around their parents. They'd gone no contact. The other ladies chose to limit their children's interaction with their parents—having boundaries, like their parents are never allowed to be alone with their kids.

As if those decisions and their memories weren't hard enough on these ladies, they also had to deal with how their extended families and communities saw them, talked to them, and gossiped about them. You see, most of the women who shared with me had never told anyone (other than their husbands) what their parents were really like. So, because of what their parents had secretly done to them, these ladies were now being talked to or about badly.

Here are some of the things these brave, beautiful, strong women had been told or overheard people say:

"But they are your parents."

"You only have one mom. You only have one dad."

"They did the best they could do."

"You'd just cut them out like that? After all they've done for you?"

"I could never do that to *my* parents."

"You'll miss them when they're gone."

"You shouldn't use your kids as weapons against your parents."

"No matter what, family should stick together."

"How could you do that to your mother?"

"You're so ungrateful!"

"You owe your parents a lot. They are both such God-fearing people."

If you were blessed with good, honest, loving parents who sacrificed for and protected you, you may subconsciously think all parents are like yours. But sadly, they're not. Before taking a side or weighing in on a situation, we must acknowledge and accept that we do not know everything. Like I said earlier, we only know what we see and what we're told. If you're aware of a situation where an adult child has gone limited or no contact with their parents, please don't make assumptions. Pray for everyone involved and please, please do not lecture anyone—you may unknowingly be punishing a victim.

Let me also address something that goes with what I've shared so far and I believe is so important for all mothers to understand. Many of these ladies' abusers were their dads. Even though it was their fathers abusing them, some of the ladies chose to go no contact with their mothers as well. Why? Because their mothers knew what was happening to them, and their mothers did not protect them.

This leads us into another difficult area. Many of their mothers were burdened by wrong biblical application. While the Bible *does* teach that God hates divorce and that husbands are the head of the home, these truths do *not* give men the right to abuse their wives and children.

This devotion was hard to write, and I know for many of you, it was hard to read. Life and relationships can truly be messy. In all the mess, please don't turn away from God. He loves you and is there to help you. Also, when looking at other people's "messes," don't turn toward your own understanding because you may *not* understand their situation at all. Lastly, do everything you can to protect yourself and your kids. If you and/or they are being abused, go to the police, tell your pastor—get help.

PRAYER PROMPTS FOR TODAY

~ Pray for those who were or are being abused.

~ We all want consequences for anyone who abuses another person, and as appropriate and justified as those re-percussions are, we must also pray for their hearts. They, too, were created by God. Pray that they will truly see the pain they've caused and the evil they've committed. Pray their hearts will be convicted and that they will turn to God.

PEACE

*Peace I leave with you; my peace I give you.
I do not give to you as the world gives. Do not let
your hearts be troubled and do not be afraid.*

John 14:27, NIV

"We just have to make it through next week, and then things will calm down." Have you ever said something like that? I have, and then typically after the next week, things *don't* slow down.

Something new always comes up. "Go, go, go!" seems to be the slogan of the world we live in now. Most of us find ourselves stressed, overwhelmed, and running on empty.

If I just had a little more money, everything would be better. Has that thought ever crossed your mind? The statement "money can't buy happiness" is definitely true, but *not* having enough money can absolutely bring unhappiness and stress.

I just can't deal with them today. Have you ever felt that way about someone? Relationships and healthy boundaries can be very difficult to maintain. The worry we feel about our loved ones' decisions, actions, and futures can keep us up at night. This leads to mental and physical exhaustion.

Our schedules, finances, and relationships all look different, but there is one thing every single one of us craves: peace. The world tells us that peace is the absence of conflict. Unfortunately, a life with absolutely no conflict isn't possible. So, does that mean a life filled with peace is also impossible?

Thankfully, the answer is no. God offers us peace that gives us a confident assurance in any circumstance. What does this look like? It looks like a woman who feels a calmness in her soul, a calmness that's rooted in her understanding that her emotions are not fed or determined by her circumstances. Her peace is found in her confidence that

God is with her and will supply everything she needs to weather every storm she faces.

Prayer Prompts for Today

~ Ask God to flood your soul with the peace that only He can give.

~ Tell God every situation that is bringing stress and worry into your life. Ask Him to give you wisdom, energy, and peace in these areas.

KNOWING GOD

Then I will give them a heart to know Me,
that I am the LORD; and they shall be
My people, and I will be their God, for they
shall return to Me with their whole heart.

Jeremiah 24:7, NKJV

One of my friends, Katelyn, shared her beautiful testimony with me yesterday. She told me that last month, she asked Jesus to be her Lord and Savior.

I was thrilled but also surprised. She and I first met about fifteen years ago. We went to church together for many years. I thought she'd given her heart to Jesus when she was a child, and for a long time, she thought so too.

Katelyn told me that for years, she thought she'd gotten saved at vacation bible school (VBS). This was my favorite thing she said: "Over this last year, I realized that I knew *about* God, but I really didn't *know* God." She told me that when she was a child at VBS, an adult put her on the spot by asking her, "Do you want to be saved?" She said she knew he wanted her to say yes, so she told him yes. She repeated a prayer he led and then was told she was saved.

Before I continue with Katelyn's testimony, let me say that Katelyn and I love VBS, and I'm thrilled to share that both of our sons were saved this year at VBS! I believe wholeheartedly that her son's and my Derek's salvation experiences were heartfelt, true, and life-changing. The night Derek accepted Christ, he told me, "I did *not* want to go forward because I didn't want people looking at me, but God told my heart that tonight was the night."

I've been blessed to have helped at more vacation bible schools than I can count. I've seen children come forward for salvation who understand exactly what they're doing. I've also seen kids who didn't fully comprehend salvation yet, and I see those experiences as moments where seeds for understanding were planted. Vacation bible schools are valuable investments into the hearts and minds of children. If you were saved at VBS, please know that if you understood and believed, your salvation experience was true and real. Now back to Katelyn's testimony.

Katelyn believed the man at VBS and thought "she was good" for almost twenty-five years until she, her husband, and their kids joined a new church. That's when God used her new pastor's sermons to convict her heart. Through his teaching, Katelyn realized she'd never experienced God's life-changing salvation. So, at thirty-two years old, she prayed and asked Jesus to be her Lord and Savior. Praise God!

After becoming a Christian, Katelyn stood before her church and let them know that she was a new child of God. She told me that as she stood in front of the congregation, her heart was pounding out of her chest and she felt a bit embarrassed because she knew some of the others there thought she'd gotten saved years ago.

My friend's story may resonate with you. It may remind you of your own experience. You, too, may know *about* God but not *know* Him personally. You may also have friends and family who already think you're a believer when you know you've never had that life-changing experience with Jesus. If this describes you, please be like my friend, Katelyn, and give your heart to God. If you'd like to do that but don't know how, please read the next devotion.

Prayer Prompts for Today

~ If you attend a church that provides a VBS to your community, please pray for the children who attend and for the workers. You may want to consider participating in VBS. Your help would be a blessing to many!

THERE IS HOPE!

For it is by grace you have been saved,
through faith—and this is not from
yourselves, it is the gift of God . . .

Ephesians 2:8, NIV

I was listening to a man share his testimony in an online video while I cooked dinner last week. One statement he made really stood out to me. He said, "Believing that God is real isn't enough.

That won't get you to Heaven. I mean, even demons believe God's real."

Dear reader, I hope and pray you *do* believe God is real and that Jesus is His Son, but to be a child of God—to be Heaven-bound—there are two more key elements to your salvation.

First, ask for God's forgiveness. We are all sinners. Romans 3:23 (KJV) teaches us, "For all have sinned, and come short of the glory of God." But there is hope! 1 John 1:9 (ESV) tells us, "If we confess our sins, he is faithful and just to forgive us our sins and to cleanse us from all unrighteousness." Second, invite God to be the Lord of your life. Ask Him to save you.

If you would like to give your heart to God and ask Him to be your Lord and Savior, hallelujah! There are no magic words to save you, no specific prayer that must be said, but I have written a salvation prayer in the following section that you are welcome to pray. There's no power in the words—the power for salvation comes from *believing* the words.

Dear God,

I come to You a sinner. I know only You can save me. I believe Jesus is the Son of God. I believe He lived a perfect, sinless life. I believe He died on a cross for my sins and arose three days later. Because of what Jesus did, I know I can have a relationship with You. God, I ask You to please forgive my sins and come into my heart. I ask You to be Lord of my life. Thank You for giving me eternal salvation that is not based on my actions. I am not perfect, and I know I never will be. No matter what mistakes I make in the future, I know I will still be saved. I will still be Yours. I know You will never leave me. Please help me to follow and trust You in every situation. Thank You for loving and forgiving me. In Jesus's name I pray, Amen.

If you meant these words,
let me be the first to congratulate you!

Welcome to the family!

Thank you for reading
Same God, New You – Book Two
If you enjoyed the book,
please leave an online review!

Scan the code to leave
a review on Amazon.

Acknowledgments

Thank you to my amazing beta readers!
Your feedback was instrumental in
shaping this book.

Alex Flora

Alana Allen

Amanda Allen

Cecelia Flora

Beth Flora

Taylor Haynie

Mary Beth Baccus

Robin McAlpin

Laurel Berry

Julie May

Allison Wilks

Megg Crane

Kylie Hawes

Special thanks to:
Julie May at Anything Creative
Natalia Leigh at Enchanted Ink Publishing

References

1. Lewis, C. S. (2015) *A Grief Observed*. HarperOne. p. 52.

2. Macdonald, George. As cited on goodreads. https://www.goodreads.com/author/quotes/2413.George_MacDonald?page=2. February 6, 2025.

3. Barrie, J. M. (2015) *Peter Pan*. HarperCollinsPublishers. p. 12.

4. As quoted on Merrian-Webster. https://www.merriam-webster.com/dictionary/grow%20up. February 6, 2025.

5. Franklin, Benjamin. *Poor Richard's Almanack*. 1733 edition.

6. Minerd, Alissa. As cited on Fred Rogers Institute. https://www.fredrogersinstitute.org/team/alissa-minerd. February 6, 2025.

7. Penn, William. (1693) Some Fruits of Solitude. As cited on Library of Congress. https://www.loc.gov/item/today-in-history/october-14/#:~:text=Time%20is%20what%20we%20want,Founding%20of%20the%20American%20Republic. February 6, 2025.

Magnolia Jane

Maggie receives an unexpected call at work, exposing a complicated family secret. In search of answers, she travels to her mother's hometown and discovers more than she was looking for. During a tense and somewhat embarrassing moment, Maggie meets a man who could possibly change her life, but a shocking accident puts their future in jeopardy. Will Maggie's story end with "happily ever after," or will she find herself alone, picking up the pieces of her dreams?

Magnolia Jane is a page-turning Christian romance full of small-town charm, heartwarming relationships, and endearing characters you'll love!

Perfect for fans of:
- Sweet Romance
- Swoon-Worthy Moments
- Found Family
- Small-Town Living
- Relatable Characters
- Family Forgiveness
  and Healing

MORE BOOKS
By Holly Jo Flora

Same God, New You

Devotions for Personal
& Spiritual Growth

JACK THE BAD CROW

JACK THE BAD CROW STRIKES AGAIN

JACK THE BAD CROW RETURNS

JACK THE BAD CROW

THE COMPLETE COLLECTION

CLAWTHORNE

A JACK THE BAD CROW STORY

Author Holly Jo Flora

Holly Jo Flora loves writing Christian romance, women's devotions, and children's fiction. She lives in Alabama with her husband and their two children.

Subscribe to Holly Jo's newsletter at hollyjoflora.com

@HollyJoFlora

www.ingramcontent.com/pod-product-compliance
Lightning Source LLC
Chambersburg PA
CBHW061801120626
46550CB00005B/2092